STEPPING STONES
VISHNU KRISTNA

© **VISHNU KRISTNA 2025**

Email: poeticxpress100@gmail.com

ISBN: 978-1-0370-3508-1(print)

978-1-0370-3509-8(e-book)

Published by SAKURA BOOK PUBLISHING
alta@sakurabookpublishing.com

All rights reserved. This publication, and no part thereof, may be reproduced in any form or by any means, electronic, mechanical, photocopying, recording, scanning, or otherwise without written permission from the author or publisher. It is against copyright law to copy this book, upload it to a website, or distribute it by any other means without the author's permission.

This book is dedicated to my late Dad, Mr. Narainsamy Kristna.

*Your memory will forever live
in the words that I write
and the way that I live.*

PREFACE

A collection of life events led to the decision to write about my circumstances in life in order to help and inspire others who are going through similar situations in their own lives. Every poem has a personal struggle that I went through on my own journey of life, and the clarity and understanding I have found in order to overcome them.

Every poem should leave the reader inspired and feeling like they can take away some life lessons from them. My aim is to help people realize that they do not have to go through struggles and problems alone and that there is always someone to talk to and help them.

This book serves as a beacon of hope for those that are lost and I hope that it leaves a positive message in the reader's hearts and minds about life, because we are all in it together and we must always strive to do our best, no matter the situation of circumstance.
With that said, read and enjoy! Thank you for your support.

A ROSE

For people a rose is just a flower merely a
means to show their affection
to me a rose is much more than that
besides being a symbol of love a rose can
also be a symbol of life

The stem could be the journey of life
and the thorns on the stem
could be the obstacles we face
but at the very top
after overcoming all of those hardships
is a beautiful rose
which represents a happy and peaceful life
showing us that if we weather the storms
there's always a light at the end of the tunnel

Whether we are looking for love or life
there's always tomorrow
and hope does exist
so the next time you look at a rose
look deeper
there's more to this beautiful creation
than what meets the eye.

POINT OF NO RETURN

I started off full of energy and zest
I always tried to be my best
I always tried to be all I could be
but nobody wanted to see the real me

Everyone tried to change me
into something they wanted me to be
but what they all failed to see
that it wasn't the real me

I've tried explaining it to them
but they failed to listen
they were happy dictating my goals
and ambitions

I accepted it for a while
thinking they were doing me good
but yearning for my dreams
was something no one else understood?
I did what they asked me to do
and I hated it but no one knew
I convinced myself that that was the way
because I knew I had no other say
I went along for a few years
despite it bringing me a lot of tears

I thought things would get better but it
was still the same I was getting older
and wiser but didn't see a change like
a lot of things in my life I was wrong
and the more it went on the less I felt
like I belonged

This cut me deep
and broke my heart
holding it together was tearing me apart
The constant humiliation was enough
turning this hopeful man towards solitude

People didn't help by fueling my anger
turning my inner peace into a stranger
the protector of the universe has set me free
enabling me even in darkness to see
for that I am eternally grateful
and I will stay forever faithful

I sometimes felt like there was no turning back
A point of no return
Where my mind was left to burn
A point where I needed to break free
And just be okay with being me

I was at the point of no return.

RED LOVE

Through the crater of a magnificent volcano
comes the deep red lava bursting to the surface
exploding in a shower of colour and light some
think of this eruption as violent and dangerous
but it could also be anger and frustration

That the volcano feels alone and forgotten
the only way for everybody to take notice of it
is if it makes a bold and grand statement
by erupting and spewing it's lava all over
by reminding people that it is still around

Nobody bothers what volcanoes can offer
some people are just taken in
by their perceptions about them
have you ever thought about
Why volcanoes erupt the way they do?
from afar a volcano may look
big and indestructible
but that is just a facade

they really have very fragile personalities
that's why they are dormant one day and
erupting the next

A volcano may seem powerful and strong
but if we look into the crater
we see that it's hollow
and that shows that it too is vulnerable
vulnerable to the elements of the people's minds
spreading false truths about them
being dangerous and violent
and that's what causes it to erupt
the inability to withstand the lies it's fed
Nobody cares to look beyond its surface
and into the heart
of this unique lava-filled friend
instead of learning more
we criticize and mock
that is what we as humans do
about the things we do not understand
we try to put a label on it

But the volcano erupts in retaliation
and there's nothing more for people to say
except that it is dangerous and hostile
that's just what people see at face value
but never judge a book by its cover

A volcano can never blend in
no matter what
it always stands out
like a diamond in a gold field however there's
not many left in the world they are an
endangered species and we are not doing
anything to save them like we would for the
plants or the animals a rare species that
people want to destroy
instead of saving them
Why?
we will never know

The next time you see a volcano
don't listen to what others have to say about it
take the time and find out for yourself
what this lava-filled friend is all about
and maybe, just maybe
you might get to see a different side of it
that nobody thought could possibly exist.

THE OCEAN BREEZE

As I sit on the soft sand and look at the
vast ocean before me my mind floats into
tranquility as I close my eyes and listen to
the waves as they kiss the shore

I lay still and feel the wind
blowing through the air
and only then do I realize
the beauty of the ocean
it is a free spirit
unhindered by rules and conformity
unbound to anything or anyone

As I sit on the ocean shore
I can feel the free spirit
splashing against my skin
and for a moment too
my spirit is set free
all from a touch
of this mysterious and magical elixir

All the negativities from my soul and spirit
are washed away and disappear

my body feels rejuvenated and my
mind is put at ease I open my eyes
and feel as alive and free as the
ocean as if it had the ability to know
all my troubles and issues and heal
them from a single touch

As night falls and moonlit skies cover the ocean
with a blanket of white light
I come to realize that the ocean
is a natural yet mysterious beauty
as its physical beauty and mystery
cannot be forged or understood by man

It has the ability to touch all your senses
and rejuvenate your soul
in unimaginable ways
that have never been felt before
its essence cannot be quantified or explained
and that's what is the mystery of the ocean
magical
serene
and always beautiful
to the senses
and to my soul.

DREAM ANGEL

When I first gazed into your eyes my heart lit
up like the sun after a stormy night piercing
my body to the depths of my soul a feeling
overcame me that has eluded me for many
years I've almost given up the search and
decided to settle alone with myself

But the divine had other plans for me
sending me an angel
in my deepest darkest hour
to transform me and heal my soul
into a man worthy enough man
for this angel before me

I feel like you are the answer
to all my hopes and dreams
revitalizing my dying soul
and breathing new life into me

Destroying the loneliness that locked
my soul in chains denying me love
and happiness keeping me
imprisoned in sadness

Now I realize that the loneliness
filled my life because my soul
was just yearning for yours
and now that I found you
I know my heart will be happy forever

Uniting our two souls together
breathing new life into my dull existence
you have brought hope and joy
into the emptiness of my soul
and love into my heart
that didn't even exist before

Every time I prayed for that someone special
I thought my prayers weren't being answered
but now I realize that I was just being prepared
so that I can be the man you always desired
and be the answer to your prayers

I am grateful and thankful
to have you in my life
and excited for all our adventures ahead
the thrilling and happiest time of my life
because I will be spending it with you

The angel of my dreams.

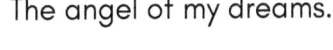

LIGHTHOUSE

Like teardrops from the heavens trickled
down onto your body forming the most
blessed of souls a soul that's more beautiful
than a rising sun on a spring morning that's
my feeling when I'm with you

A rainbow after a tremendous storm
a storm that has filled me
with constant uncertainty
like a ship that's lost at sea
and you a lighthouse beacon
We discovered each other
Miraculously and timeously

Guiding me to safety
nurturing my body and soul
showing me the way
in the treacherous storm of my life
directing my soul towards yours
with the light of your heartbeat
being my only guide

that is the power of your love

As it comes from a beautiful soul that is so strong and sturdy like a lighthouse every minute of every day your essence draws my soul closer to yours promising not to lead me astray and holding me in your beautiful glow.

A FRIENDSHIP POEM

What makes us human? it is the ability to show
compassion for one another when we share
this energy with someone it ignites our souls

and fills our entire being with passion this
incredible energy is known as love

Love can be expressed in many ways
and can be felt in even more
love fills me with happiness
when I am feeling down
love holds my hand
when I don't want to walk alone
love gives me an entire book
when all I needed was a page

love lends me a shoulder to lean on
when I can't stand on my own two feet
love is my true friend indeed

When I really needed inspiration
in my time of strife
I prayed to the heavens to save my life
they answered my call
and shone down on me

sending an angel to set me free there's
not a day that goes by without me
thanking them for hearing my cry and
sending me a very special friend one
who I will love till the very end

A woman with so much compassion in her
that it overflows onto me
without a care

one with the sweetest of smiles

that can be seen for many a mile
brightening the streets
wherever she walks

and making the most melodious sound

when she talks
her beautiful voice
travels directly to my soul
she speaks to my heart
igniting it
energizing it
breathing new life into it

A friendship with you is so inspiring
it has helped me to grow as a person
without it I know my life would worsen
you taught me to be more caring
and more understanding

You know there's a famous saying with a lover you can share many things but with a friend you can share everything that encompasses our relationship of which I am forever grateful.

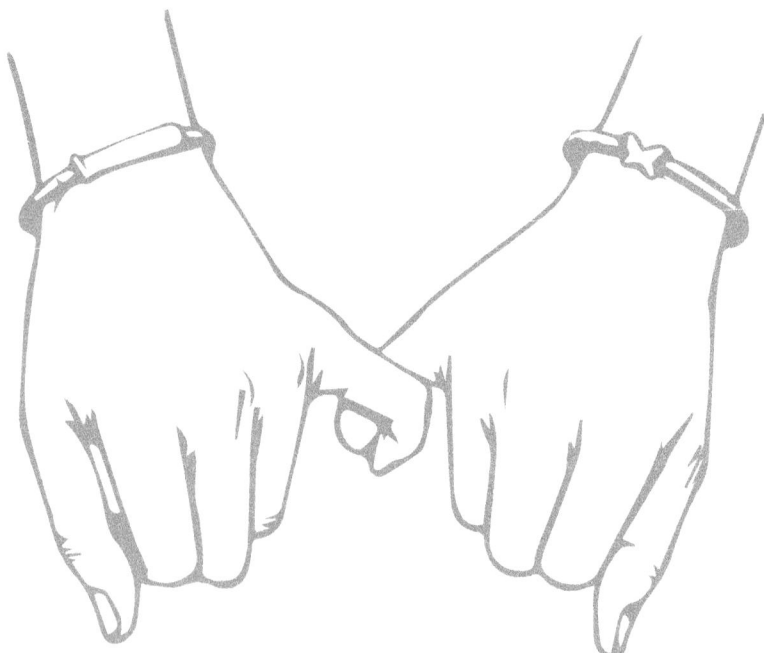

EPITOME

All my sensory pleasures converge on you with
every glimpse as though anew sending my
senses to new heights of pleasure you are by far
my greatest treasure a simple smile washes all
my worries away
turning to sunshine all the clouds of grey

The mountains of life you help me climb
helping me through all my trying times
I wonder what would I be without you?
my whole world would crumble
louder than thunder
and the lightning would strike the mountain
with such force
that my life
would result in absolute chaos

You are more precious to me
than the most precious stone
and not a step will I take
if I am to do it alone
your golden smile sets my heart on fire
because you are my strongest desire
life without you
would not be the same for me
Who would be the same?

after they've been sent a heavenly angel
I've never really understood love
till the day that I met you
I've just been lonely
sad and blue
you've brightened up my days
with your sunshine
and ended them with sunsets
that are glorious and divine
like a rainbow after the storm
you breathed new life
in a beautiful new form
The essence of your existence
takes my breath away
you are my dream come true
in every single way
a moment without you
seems like a lifetime
but a moment with you
makes everything feel right
your gentle caress
embraces my soul
you make me happy
you make me whole
you are the epitome
of everything I want and need.

DESTINATION

Trying to touch the hand of the living
hoping that it would be more forgiving
for I have been reaching all my life to
end this toxic eternal strife

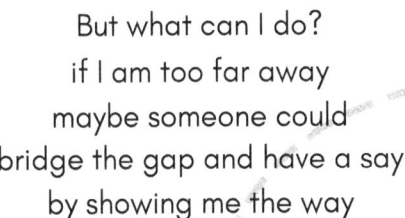

But what can I do?
if I am too far away
maybe someone could
bridge the gap and have a say
by showing me the way

Just a thought that I always find
that this lonely town has left me in a bind
there's only so many places to find salvation
this vast limitation leads to starvation
starvation of the mind
body and soul
I search for a way to feel completely whole

It is a privilege and an honor
to meet such inspiration
with desire and dreams
stopped by no limitation
and not corrupt with imitation

Full of hope
I buy a ticket to the big city
but the bus seems to be filled
with such negativity
the queue for the bus is very long
maybe it's a sign
that maybe I'm wrong

Maybe I've been fooling myself
all these years
which stopped me
from moving on
and facing my fears
it is difficult
when you're learning on your own
how to live your life
while facing the unknown

I believe that the journey you take
is greater than the destination
and the way we handle
our everyday situation
when we reach our destination
will determine whether
we will finally feel free
I hope that it will all pay off and be worth it
that I cannot guarantee.

IF

If you don't want to smile then
how can I make you laugh

If you don't want to hear me
then how can I speak my mind

If you don't teach me
then how will I learn
If you don't give me a chance
then how will I prove myself

If I can't tell you
how you truly make me feel today
then how will you ever know

If I can't share my dreams with you
then how can I turn them into reality

If I can't feel your sweet lips against mine
then how will I know
if you feel the same way too

If you could only see through my eyes
what I see when I look at you then you
might understand my desire

If you could only feel the surge
that runs through my entire body
every time you're near me

If only you were mine for real
instead of just on my mind

If only.

SENSUOUS MELODIES

The sound of your sweet voice is
like music to my soul it leaves me
feeling complete and whole

your angelic voice moves through the air
penetrating my ears
with utmost care it enters my
body until it fills my entire being

And I wonder?
if it's real
what I'm hearing
then I realize
that it is the power of your voice
the sweet sounds
don't really give me a choice

The power of your voice
is ever so strong
that it fills my heart
and takes away everything wrong
it ignites my soul
with a blazing fire
that strengthens
my deepest compassion and desire
as I dive into an ocean

of sweet melodious sound I feel as
though I'm not earth-bound

I wonder to myself
Where can I be?
I am in your soul
peaceful and free
exploring all your passions and desires
cutting through all the delicate wires
of time and space
looking at each other
face to face

As two become one
I slowly discover
your essence and being
truly remarkable
all the things that I'm feeling
I never knew that I could feel this way
I just wish that we could fly away
high above and into the sky
where we wouldn't have a burden
or worry
or ever shed a tear
we'd simply be together
now and forever.

TEARDROPS

As teardrops trickle down my face I feel
as though I'm in a strange place a river of
tears floods my soul leaving me feeling
incomplete and not whole

What can I ever do?
to change this predicament
I'm a rock in the deepest cave covered by
numerous layers of sediment it seems as though
I have nowhere to run to every destination
has the same situation and similar people too

As the passing days seem more difficult to
handle I try to reignite my life's candle like
a movie that always has a beginning and
an end and the plot is my life
that's always in a twist and bend

So many thoughts buzz through my mind
but when I search I
cannot find
every day starts and ends the same way
it's as though I have zero say

People always want to change me
seems they don't like what they hear and see
I cannot change the way I am
my mind feels like a thousand pebbles
tossed in a huge dam

I try my best to cover the pain
to show them sunshine instead of rain
I feel when I speak that nobody listens
the look at my eyes gleams with anticipation
as it glistens
Instead of lending me some support
I get angry and frustrated
and have little to no thought
I have nobody who understands me
to help me be
all that I can be

It seems as though I'm a leaf in a river swaying from side to side waiting for someone to deliver me but nobody wants to help the real me it seems that's the one person they cannot see me that's why I'm drowning in my teardrops.

LONGING

The intensity of our meetings grows
stronger every day so I pray to God to
show me the way to your heart and your
soul to make me feel complete and whole

I know that patience is a virtue
sometimes loneliness overpowers all

I must be stronger and try not to rush
for our meeting is something
I long for very much

I dream about you all the time
and I'm hoping that you're doing the same
even though I don't know what you look like
I feel that your spirit and mine are alike

I long to meet you
and feel a love so true
I know that you're a precious gem
whose love nobody can condemn

I hope that God sends you a sign
to tell that you will forever be mine
that your heart belongs to me
as mine does to you

Let us hope and anticipate the meeting
of two destined hearts and two souls
forever entwined through the journey of
life's mystery

I hope these words find a way into your heart
and gives you hope
that our meeting
is the only thing that keeps us apart
and when we do meet
and have that connection
then we will realize the cosmic intervention

That our meeting was meant to be
more than either of us anticipated
a blessing from God
to our respective hearts.

ALLURE

With a gentle caress of those delicate lips
I'm sent into a deeper state of sheer bliss I
find myself getting deeper and deeper
my heart is the treasure
and you are its keeper

You are a ray of light
that shines straight into my heart
two souls entwined in the mystery of life
living and loving each other
for eternity
Exploring the deepest part of your mind
the vulnerable place
that you only let those closest to you enter
only those that are truly closest
to your heart and soul
the place that I would love to take a journey to
every time I look
into your captivating, soulful eyes

Every night as you lay yourself down to sleep
I sit beside you
and I watch you sleeping so peacefully
and I wonder to myself

How did I ever summon an angel from heaven?
To come down and lay here beside me It's been
quite a while and I still can't believe it

It's just that I'm amazed by you
you are a remarkable woman
It's your style
your personality
your mystique

Just everything about you leaves me breathless
they say beauty is in the eye of the beholder
but you're a beauty for the ages.

A TRIBUTE TO MY MOTHER

What can be said about a person
who endured so much
to bring me into this world Mum, you
have been there for me my entire
life and I thank you words can't
express how much you mean to me

the sacrifices you made for me
will never be forgotten they are
appreciated and will always
remind me of how much you
care for me

That's what makes you such a remarkable
and special person to me
you never pretended to care for me
what you did came straight from your heart
and for that I am eternally grateful.

I know that my world
is much better because of you
and as I get older
I begin to realize the true value of a mother

Nobody can ever replace you and nobody would ever care for me the way that you do I realized that a mother's love is like no other on earth I am grateful for every moment that we share together.

You are my shoulder to lean on
when I need one
you are there to lend an ear
when I need someone to listen
you are there to help me
when I can't help myself
you understand me
like nobody else does

you are my mother,
and I love you very much.

May God grant you many more days on earth to share many more special moments with me.

TRUE FRIEND

Brave soul that has no boundaries in assisting and comforting those in the most trying of times reassuring you that everything will be fine even in your darkest hour of need encouraging and uplifting you to your highest potential without having anything to gain never discouraging you on your weaknesses but always mentioning your strengths

Dynamic and powerful are the words that enter your mind and resonate within your soul open to every aspect of your personality and character without harsh judgment naturally communicating to your mind always instilling words of wisdom for your growth

Joyful and happy is always the after-effect of being in their company even for a moment open to listening to your problems and offering advice without any judgment strong-willed and unwavering connection that enhances your soul to its highest potential

Enlightening you
with true knowledge and wisdom
so that you may prosper in this world
persevering in their plight to assist you
no matter how dire the consequences
humility from their heart
is so great and strong
that it overflows directly in your soul.

That is a true friend indeed
through the good times
sad times
and bad times
someone that you can count on
who will always be there for you by your side
without any condemnation

Why, you may ask?
because a true friend is just that
true to your heart and your soul
with the best intentions for you

Remember if you do find that true friend
treasure them with all your heart
because they only come around
once in a lifetime.

MY FUTURE PARTNER

Patience has been a virtue that I have carried
knowing that God will eventually lead me
on the path of my destiny to you
even though it has been lonely
and unbearable at times
I never gave up hope
in the belief that God
would never fail me in my pursuit
to find my one true love

When I first saw you and looked directly
into your soulful eyes
I knew at that moment
that my prayers were answered
and that I had found my soulmate
someone with a beautiful soul
that I have been praying for my entire life
I knew that I had found my home
a home of refuge and of comfort
filled with trust
and understanding
with an abundance of unconditional love

It made me so ecstatic
and full of joy in my heart that prayers to
God are never in vain and when he finally
decided to bless me with somebody that
was everything I ever dreamt of and ever
wanted in a partner then I knew I had
found my soulmate

A partner that made me realize
that everything I've ever been through
and endured in my life
no matter how difficult at times
was unfortunate but necessary
in order for me to truly appreciate
and value you as a the person
after all
how can you truly appreciate
love and compassion
unless you have been through
the hurt and pain
how can you truly appreciate your soulmate
unless you know the torment
of being lost and alone for so long

As an added bonus
you have really gotten me closer to God
as I now totally believe
that nothing or no request is beyond him

No matter how difficult
or impossible it may seem
to us God's word simply put is that nothing
is impossible with him and the fact that we
are here together
is a testament to that fact

It still astounds me
that he sent me a soulmate
with such a kind
caring
and loving soul
with the most beautiful heart
that I have experienced in my entire life

You were definitely worth the wait
and you have breathed new life
into my mind,
body and soul, energizing it
rejuvenating it in a way
that no other person has ever done before

I can't wait to start this journey with you
and anticipate all the wonderful
and memorable adventures

that we will share together I'm sure
that those adventures will not last a
lifetime but an eternity because I trust
in our love I trust in our commitment I
trust in our belief but most of all I trust
in our God that he will lead our way
through life's winding path and that he
will always be before us behind us and
above us protecting us and guiding us

Everything that I've been through in life
all the ups and downs
all the highs and lows
has been worth it in hindsight
because that journey
has allowed our paths to cross in this life
and I am eternally grateful
and thankful to God
for sending me an angel
to love and bless my life

So I want to thank you my love
for allowing God to guide you

in your journey of life and since our love was ordained by God our hearts were spiritually connected long before we ever knew each other because his divine presence has a plan guiding our hearts together to be spiritually and eternally connected and now I can rejoice in the power of love but more importantly in the power of God.

HEARTBEATS

As blood courses through my veins with
every heartbeat I am drawn closer to
your vibrant and energetic soul ever
since we met and became closer it
seems as though the rhythm of my
heartbeat changed

Changed into a different rhythm
a rhythm that is either slowing down
or speeding up
only when you were close to me
did I realize what was happening
as I felt your heartbeat against mine

I was amazed
that they were both beating in synchronicity
together as one
because when two souls connect
and share so much with each other
even their hearts begin to beat as one
and acclimatize to each other
and when that happens
they cannot live without each other

Because they share a heartbeat
making them want to always be close
and connected with each other as
hearts that beat as one can never be
too far from each other for too long
otherwise they will start to slow down
steadily decreasing out of sync
ever so slightly with each new day

Why, you may ask?
because they don't have their heartmate to
energize their hearts
and the way they do this
is simply by placing their heart on yours
and the energy and love
they feel for each other
ignites their hearts.
rejuvenating their pulse rate
and synchronizing their heart beats once again
simply by loving someone

You are unknowingly
keeping each other alive
because the heart needs love
to grow and connect on a deeper level
and that also increases
your understanding of life

Giving it a deeper intense meaning
Remember
just as the body needs exercise
to grow stronger
the heart needs love
affection
and kindness
to grow and prosper
you have filled my heart
with so much of positivity and love
that it is overflowing
through my entire body and soul
reaching places that I never knew existed
and igniting my spirit
with every single
Heartbeat.

TIME

Our time on this earth is defined and limited
nobody knows how much time they have
so instead of promoting
the negativity in our lives
like anger frustration stress
and loss

why don't we instead choose
to exhibit positive qualities
like love
happiness
and humility

During your limited time here
do all the things that make you happy
because you never know
when you will run out of time
and always remember tomorrow
is not promised to anybody
so make the best of today
be present in the moment
with every fiber of your being
Remember to seize the opportunity
of the present
and tell someone that you love them

showing someone that you love and care for them
is one of the best things that you can do

Loving someone is never wrong
if it comes from your heart
love from the heart
is having the best intentions for someone
and is also food for your soul

Loving someone is one of the best experiences
that our limited time on earth offers
unconditional love is one of the purest
and most divine expressions in this world
it will make your time here the most exciting
giving you the memorable moments
of your existence
it will bring out the best in you
and increase the way
you experience your time on earth
in ways that you have never imagined
or thought possible

Love breaks all boundaries
and elevates our levels of existence
it's the way God wanted us to exist
and interact in this world
by showing each other love
by truly and unconditionally loving someone

you are honoring God and living the way he intended us to so take that leap of faith and change your life because we really don't have much time left on earth.

STRENGTH

Physical strength is not built overnight
athletes train for numerous years to build
muscle, flexibility and endurance whereas
inner strength is built by positive affirmations
words of encouragement showing and
receiving love and caring for people

Mind strength is when you know your worth
and you never let anyone
treat you in an unworthy manner

Mind strength is when you treat yourself
with a certain level of respect
you never allow or tolerate anyone
being disrespectful to you

Mind strength is when
you love yourself completely
you never allow anyone
to mistreat or abuse your love

Mind strength is when you place
the needs of others above your
own you feel happy and content
that you made a difference in
someone else's life

Mind strength is when
you don't need to validate yourself
with expensive clothes and shoes
the value of yourself is seen by others
through the content of your character

Mind strength is when
you are willing to except change
and being corrected when you are wrong
by not being in denial or rigid in your ways
thinking you are always right

Mind strength is when
you think you love someone
but choose to walk away from the relationship
because it doesn't satisfy you emotionally
or uplift you spiritually
it drains you physically
and leaves you feeling down
after spending time with them

Mind strength is when you can forgive someone
who has hurt you in the most destructive way
even though you carry the weight of that hurt on
your shoulders on a daily basis you show
compassion and love to everyone in your world

Mind strength is when you can truly love
trust and care for another person again
after your heart has been shattered
into a million tiny pieces previously

That shows true strength
Unwavering strength
Inspiring strength
Godly strength!

THE DISADVANTAGED

Judgment on others through
your perceived view is a
reflection of oneself Judgment
in this world is reserved for one
and one only that is God

People attach so much of value on status
based on the clothes they wear
the vehicle they drive
and the residence they live at
they are consumed by material wealth
so much emphasis is placed
on attaining things of this world
to be successful
that they lose focus
on what really matters
in our lives
To be successful in life
we simply need to focus our attention on God
He will bestow upon us
the richness of his blessings
we need to believe in him
in order to receive from him
in this world it seems that status

is more important than goodness
People focus on attaining material things
to make them happy
but this form of happiness is temporary
it soon fades away
and in order to feel happy again
the endless cycle
of acquiring more things begins again

To be truly content
your heart needs to be filled with joy
the only way to get joy
is from doing joyous things
like worshipping the Lord
and giving to others less fortunate
as the hands that give are far greater
than the hands that receive
the joy received from God is not temporary
but rather ever flowing
like a never ending river flowing
directly into your heart and soul

Never look down on someone
that has lesser material wealth than you
and never look up to someone
that has more material wealth than you
those things are of this world
and it is temporary

rather seek God, who will give you eternal
joy and so much more God always has the
best reserved for you

Never judge anyone based on face value
until you have walked a day in their shoes
you never know what someone
is dealing with on the inside
never assume things about them or judge them
based on the external view
created by your own perceptions
an important sentiment
is that looks can be deceiving
The only one with the right to judge is God
that right is reserved for him
and him alone
A person may not have material wealth
but they may be fantastic artists
their drawings or paintings
may take you on such breath-taking journey
that it can only be described as extraordinary
or maybe they are a great singer
and when they sing
the amazing sound of their voice
touches your soul
and makes your heart weep

If it was not for your assumptions on people covered by your vale of perceptions then you could see people for who they really are and that is as a child of God

Everyone in life has the potential to improve and be a better version of themselves rather see the potential in someone and have empathy for them and never judge a book by its cover.

DEPRESSION

It feels like a plague that has infested your
mind destroying lively crops of your thoughts

and replacing them with sadness and negativity
there is no escape from this hollow feeling
that has hijacked your mind it feels like your
entire body is bound with chains and
shackled in an unforgiving prison

You see everything
as dull, hopeless and void of excitement
the sound of this silence
is deafening and unbearable
it engulfs your senses with negativity
and preys on your heart
like a lion stalking a gazelle
it unforgivingly tortures your mind
with every waking hour

You feel as though
you are in a dark and gloomy cave
in which no light can enter
where the darkness blinds you to a point
where all you can distinguish are sounds

Your strength feels like it is being drained from
your body and it forms puddles on the floor you
become powerless and can do nothing but allow
this affliction to take over your body and mind

Your mind feels like it's stuck in a maze
alone and helpless
with nobody to save your soul
I scream at the top of my lungs
with all the strength I can muster
but there's no reply
it attacks my senses
like a powerful and strategic army
easily destroying all my defenses
overpowering my body and mind
until I am conquered
and reduced to nothing

What the enemy didn't realize at that moment
I was down but I was not fully defeated
they have captured my body
but my mind was not fully shut down
as they had expected
summoning up all the strength and courage
that I could muster
I let out one last deafening cry for help

that shocked everyone around me and they came to my assistance not to pick me up but to raise their hands instead They stood around me in prayer as I lay there confused as they continued to pray I gained more strength enough to let out another bellowing cry for help but this time I added another word at the end Help me, Jesus!

A bright light overcame me and released me
from the chains that bound my mind
every darkness in my entire being
was flooded with bright white light
I experienced reverent peace and relief
in my heart like never before
and I knew and felt that I was free
and I owe it all to the Lord Jesus Christ

Thank you, Jesus.

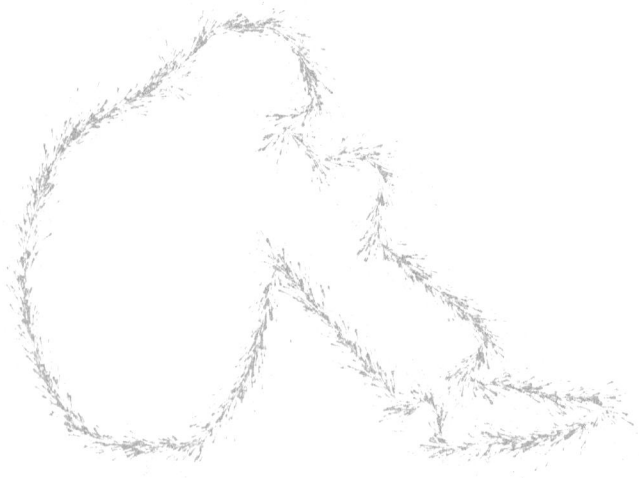

TRACING

Somebody that accepts me for who I am
unconditionally expecting nothing in return
nothing except love, respect and appreciation
and reciprocates that to me ten-fold somebody
that can turn my sad moments into joy by simply
being themselves with inspiring words of
encouragement motivation and upliftment

Somebody that pulls on my heartstrings
every time we communicate
without being extraordinary
by simply being themselves
that is exactly what I need
to fill my heart with joy
that it overflows
into every aspect of my existence

When we communicate
we are not bound by the confines of time
hours seem like minutes
and minutes seem like special and exclusive
moments in time

as we travel on an adventurous journey
with only our minds a person that uplifts
my spirits simply with their voice

When I'm failing to think positive
and feel positive for myself
she can feel my pain
even though we are miles apart
we don't share a superficial connection
but a deeper heart connection
and an even greater soul connection

That connection is based on friendship
love
understanding
and trust
somebody that I can laugh with when I'm happy
and will shed a tear with me
in times of strife
somebody that puts God first
in everything they do
and has total trust and belief in him
somebody that I admire and respect
because they believe in God's plan for their life

I never believed in soulmates
that is until I met you
when two souls connect

on the level that we have it must have come
from a higher power that power being God
Soulmates have so much in common with each
other they know each other's thoughts and
feelings without even uttering a word

A soulmate
will always have your best interests at heart
even if it hurts them deep inside
a soulmate is one that God has sent to me
somebody that is worth more
than all the riches in the world
the value you bring to me
cannot be diminished
unlike wealth
and wealth doesn't matter
when you have a soulmate
as they enrich your heart

Filling it with love, joy and contentment
I thank God every day
for sending me a remarkable person
that I can call my soulmate
and for blessing my life with you.

BLIND MAN

Gazing into her captivating eyes I'm drawn to your soul like a magnet it pulls me closer and grows stronger every time you stare back into mine I am picked up by your carriage of love and taken on a journey into your mind traveling through every desirable and ecstatic destination on the highway of your mind

Every smile and caring attitude from you
propels my carriage
faster to my final destination
that destination being your soul
where I will dwell
in ecstasy for my entire life
knowing that I could visit heaven
without dying
is only possible with you
happily basking in the radiant glow
of the deepest part of your being

I never want to leave
this beautiful and ecstatic state
because my heart would stop beating
without your presence in my life
I would definitely cease to exist

because you are my everything I will do anything
and everything in my power
to stay deep inside your soul
and I always oblige to satisfy every desire of
yours to the utmost of my ability

When you are unhappy or discontent
with anything you think is wrong
then I know that the heaven of our soul
will quickly turn into the hell
and my soul will burn to ashes
but when you are satisfied and happy with me
then I can be at ease
I know I've paid my rent
to reside in your soul
for another moment

I can feel so lonely and abandoned without you
it's like my heart can't function
and is shutting down
even my soul starts to cry and weep
as I don't have you next to me
I begin to wonder
how could I have been so careless
to not cater to the needs of someone
that I loved and cared for
and I make a vow to myself
to never make another mistake
or I will be thrown out

of her ecstatic love for good

Love has taken over my entire being
I cannot think or see
past your beauty and your love
I cannot imagine going a day without you
bestowing your presence on me
even if it's for just five minutes
because when we are alone
everyone else fades away
like water over a fresh palette
all the colours blend into one
none of them are as beautiful and enticing
as you are to me

I know in my heart
that nobody can be as beautiful
and captivating as you
in the entire world
I love the way that everything about you
needs to be perfect and suit your ways
because perfection demands perfection
and as I am drawn into your soul
I realize tha I am so deep in
that I can't even see where I am

It is so dark here The only thing I can see is my beautiful woman and her captivating love oblivious to anyone or anything else

I am truly a Blind Man.

MY FUTURE PARTNER

Being grateful brings a lot of ecstatic moments
to one's life sometimes these moments surprise
you as they are better than you ever expected
moments occur that make you feel like every
prayer prayed and every wish wished was
granted to me and that's how I felt when I first
saw you and looked into your captivating eyes

I never expected to see someone
that is so dedicated to the Lord
it inspired me to be a better person as well
I thank you for that from the bottom of my heart

When I look into your eyes
it's like looking at a breathtaking sunset
overlooking the blue ocean
it's beautiful to look at alone
but it's more meaningful
when sharing it with somebody

I would love to share a sunset with you
while holding you in my arms that would
make that simple experience the most
beautiful in my life because I shared it
with you the most beautiful and caring
person that I've ever met

As you turn to me and I look into your eyes
they hypnotize me
and I am taken on a journey
a journey into the deepest part
of your soulful heart
all I see are the moments
that you were happy
sad, hurt and disappointed
and also the moments
that made you laugh and cry

I don't know why you went through
those moments in your life
only God knows the reason
but I can tell you
I never want to see you shed a tear of sadness
only a tear of joy
I never want to hear the sound of your crying
I only want to hear the echoes of your laughter

I never want you to feel unsafe
I just want to hold you in my arms for protection

I never want you to feel I'm distant
because I will always keep my heart
close to yours

The reason I will do all this
I care for you with all my heart
and it would mean so much to me
if you felt the same way too.

LONELINESS

The loneliness I sometimes feel is so quiet and silent
yet it can be so deafening so deafening that I can't
even listen to my own thoughts It engulfs all my
senses taking me on a turbulent journey

A journey that travels
through all the negative emotions
I have ever felt
I try to deviate from the negative journey
into something pleasant
I'm unable to do so as I realize
I'm no longer in the driving seat of my mind
I have no option
but to continue this rollercoaster of emotions
Weaving and winding
through the traffic of my thoughts

The speed that I'm travelling at increasing rapidly
I scream in silence
fearful for my life
unable to stop this runaway wave
of negative emotions
I can barely see
in which direction I am travelling

I decided to just close my eyes and
concentrate and pray though I may not make
it through this journey alive I trust that my
Lord knows better than me as to why I am
going through this journey

I pray sincerely to the Lord
to please help me out of this situation
As I awaken on my bed
Covered in a blanket of white light
The fear and adrenaline subside
from my body and mind
as my heart rate begins to slow down
I realize I am alive
and I'm thankful to the Lord
for taking me out of my situation

The situation and struggle of loneliness
that has been with me for decades
Only you Lord know the pain and heartache
this heart, mind and body has endured
now that it has finally been released from my soul
after decades of struggle
I am eternally thankful to you Lord
For ending my loneliness.

DAD

was born into this world with an innocent heart and mind
carried from the nursery by you placed into the safe
embrace of my mother's arms you used to look at me with
caring eyes throughout the years I used to believe that I
could always count on you for anything I needed

It used to be the case until I completed high school
then everything changed
like day turns to night
so too did your feelings change towards me

I wanted to pursue a certain profession
and wasn't allowed to pursue that field
when you made up your mind
nobody could convince you otherwise
not even your wife

My heart slumped when I couldn't study what I
wanted to and so began my life of uncertainty

My dad was very controlling
and dominating in nature
he liked it when people listened to him
I was stuck for years trying to please him
but while pleasing him
I was slowly losing myself
Without even realizing it

I was not living a life of passion and happiness
but of servitude, sadness and discontentment
My dad had such a stronghold on my life
that I couldn't do anything
without his approval
and since his approval was rarely given
we didn't see eye to eye
but in order to gain and keep his approval
I decided to not retaliate and just keep the peace
that conformation caused me to just give in
and withdraw from everything

The hurtful words he used to call me
still echo in my head up to this day
it changed me as a person
I developed a low self-esteem
and was unsure of myself

as a result of his emotional abuse I felt
like I wasn't good enough as a person
to have friends to have a relationship
to have love
I mean how could someone love me
when my own father didn't

This carried on for many years
and when my dad passed away
I knew that I needed to move pass this
through a friend I went to church
and found my salvation in Jesus Christ
it transformed me
Christ says don't carry all your burdens
but just lay them at my feet
and I will carry them for you

I was going to church and worshipping God
I noticed that my confidence increased
my strength and wisdom increased
and I was building my self esteem

God says honour your parents I
cannot have any resentment or
unforgiveness towards you Dad

If you were here
I would tell him these few things

Dad, what you had put me through
had really hurt me emotionally and mentally
to the point where I saw no way out
where I found no use in living anymore
if it wasn't for Jesus saving me
I wouldn't even be here right now
Now that I am saved
and continue to grow on a daily basis
I can say that the man
who was once a broken man and sad man
a man with no passion or desire for life
has been transformed
with purpose and direction
and I hope for a better future for me
by the grace of Jesus Christ

I have grown stronger and wiser
confident in my abilities as a man
in my constant improvements as a man

I can confidently tell you that I forgive you
from the bottom of my heart for everything
that you have done knowingly or unknowingly
because forgiveness is not only for you but
more for me so that I don't need to carry this
hurt and pain anymore I can be free

I don't hold any ill-feelings towards you
you were my dad
and I wouldn't be on this earth
if it wasn't for you
I pray for God to have mercy on your soul
and for your soul to rest in peace.

I love you Dad and thank you.

FORGIVENESS

Forgiveness is the most difficult thing to do
to someone that has wronged you
it is one of the most necessary things to do
to have peace in your life
because when you forgive someone
you take the power back from the person
that wronged you
and you restore it
back to your heart and soul

Whether people have hurt you
or someone you love
forgive them
Whether people have lied to you
forgive them
Whether people have cheated on you
forgive them

Whether people have tormented and abused you
forgive them
Whether people have deceived you
forgive them
Whether people have bullied you at school
forgive them

Forgiveness will unburden your heart and soul
and set you free

If you don't forgive your perpetrators
then you will live in anger
resentment
and bitterness
for the rest of your life
as you will carry their burden on your shoulders

Forgive those that have wronged you
and leave them for God to deal with
just as Jesus Christ was being tormented
through the streets of Rome
and placed on the cross at Cavalry
he was not in anger
resentment
or hatred
but simply said the words:
"Forgive them, father, for they know not what they do"

Follow in the footsteps of the living God
and forgive anyone that has wronged you
only then will you be able to move forward
in life and find peace within yourself

only then will you be able to open your heart in
a loving way again only then will you be able to
live in joy again

And I promise you
when you forgive someone
it will feel as though a huge weight
will be lifted off your body and soul
and peace will overcome your entire being

Remember God has created us for greater things
so don't block your greatness from God
by having a bitter heart
with no room for forgiveness

Forgive the worst that has been done to you
and allow God's greatness
into your heart and soul
then watch your life
be transformed for the better
in unimaginable ways

THE ONE

Knowing the correct and right one for you is
something that everyone in this world desires
sometimes the one that you feel is the one turns out to
be something very different from what you expected

The moment you realize that somebody
is the one for you
is the moment that you know
this person encompasses
all that you ever wanted
and dreamt of in a person

It is a feeling of contentment
a feeling of protection
a feeling of security
a feeling of trust
a feeling of joy in your heart
whenever you spend time with them
it's a feeling of love
that nobody else has ever made you feel
being with them encourages you
to be best version of yourself

The one will change you subconsciously to improve yourself to be the best that you can be and they do this without any effort or strain on you they will constantly be on your mind and no matter what you are doing thinking of them will always put a smile on your face

You want to be with them
no matter how much time is spent together
because time flies when you're together
the one will always uplift you
when you are feeling down
they will always shed a tear for you
when you are feeling sad
they are always caring toward you
and they will always dry your tears
They will stand by you
no matter how difficult the situation
and never give up on you
no matter the circumstances
the one will never ever put you down
mock you
laugh at you
or make you a joke
as they truly care about you

and your well-being they will always
make time for you and want to spend
time with you the activity doesn't matter
as long as the both of you are together

The one will always want you to succeed
and will always drive you
to be the best version of yourself
encouraging you in all aspects of your life
the one will always have God
as the basis of the relationship
and know that God is the leader and director
of the relationship
The one will appreciate you
and respect you unconditionally
and never try to make you feel less than yourself
the one will always put you
above family and friends
and they will want everyone to know
that you are in a relationship

They will be proud to be with you
and never hide away from anyone
the one will always represent
unconditional true love in your life
and want nothing from you
except love in return

The one is a gift from God and is a
reward from heaven and is more
precious than all the riches of the
world as they enrich your heart and
soul and that lasts for an eternity

When you find the one
thank God
appreciate, respect, and love them
knowing that God has rewarded you
with his choicest blessings

For those of you
that haven't found the one as yet

never give up
because they are out there
ask God for guidance
and never get misled
by people pretending to be the one

A way to know if someone is pretending
they won't fulfill any of the things
that I wrote about in this poem
and they won't fill your heart with love

So go out there
find the one for yourself
because you deserve it
and you heart will love you for it!

JESUS MY SAVIOUR

God of the highest and rivalled by no other
the King of Kings and the Lord of Lords
befitting for a God you love

You died on the cross
for the sins of all mankind
and saved humanity from destruction
we are thankful
blessed
and favored
to have Jesus Christ in our lives

No problem is too big to overcome
and no mountain is too high
for you to go over for you
my Lord,
you have made the ultimate sacrifice for us
and ask nothing in return
except to praise and worship you unconditionally
and follow your ten commandments

You are the lion of Judah
and you roar
with unlimited power destroying any evil spirits
that may try to conquer your servants
you accept anyone and everyone
with open arms and a loving heart

no matter their background or past afflictions
You have authority over your disciples
you watch over and guide them
through the ups and downs of their lives
never forsaking them
you reward your obedient servants
with favoured blessings
blessings they never even dreamt possible

No matter how dire a situation can be
you can overturn it
you have the power to turn the impossible
into the possible
you can turn the natural into the supernatural
superseding anything
in any of your disciple's life
that is the power of Jesus Christ

Faith in Jesus is like food for your soul
and each prayer that you pray
and each song that you sing to worship
will fill and energize your soul
and his favour will overflow into your life

When you feel you are alone
and have nobody to talk to
know that you are not alone
because Jesus is always by your side

even though you may not recognize it he
is always there waiting for you to
acknowledge him so talk to him because
he is the best friend that you could ever
have He is the only one that can help you
when nobody else can
Jesus gives you hope when you lack it
he breathes new life in you
when you have given up on life
and don't want to go on
he lifts you up and carries you
when you can't walk on your own two feet
He is a Savior in every sense of the word

He has given us the Holy Bible to read from
to learn from his teachings
to use them as a guide to live our lives
and the more we read the word of God
the more we keep
the spirit of Jesus alive in all of us
and that brings us closer to the lord, our God

The Lord is my Savior if it wasn't for him I wouldn't be alive right now He spoke to me during my darkest hour when all my hope was lost and I didn't see any way out He spoke to me in the most commanding yet loving voice and he showed me the way out when I had lost all believe and hope

From hopelessness
to being hopeful for the future
from blinding sadness to joyous happiness
from uncertainty and anxiety
to peace and serenity
that is why I follow the Lord with all my heart

The Lord walks before me
and directs my path correctly
the Lord walks behind me
and pushes me forward
the Holy Spirit is in me
and guides my thoughts and actions
the blood of Jesus covers me
and absolves me from all my sins

The love of Jesus is knowing that He
loves me unconditionally and
He forgives my mistakes unconditionally

For those that do not follow the Lord Jesus
are always susceptible
to the workings of the devil
follow the Lord
and be set free
from all negativity and bondages
of this world
the reward is living for eternity
in the kingdom of heaven

Hallelujah and Amen.

ABOUT THE AUTHOR

Vishnu Kristna writes inspirational poetry on a variety of topics. He was born in Durban and lived in Tongaat during his early years. He then moved to a small town, Ixopo, made famous by the author Alan Paton's book, *Cry, the Beloved Country*. Ixopo was central in giving Vishnu his unique perspective and style of writing based on small-town living.

He now lives in Durban and has a Bachelor of Commerce Degree specializing in Marketing. Despite the marketing Degree and while working in online sales, he has decided to follow his passion and desire of writing and publish his first book, *Stepping Stones*.

Follow Vishnu Kristna on TikTok for more information on future projects @vish_zn or drop an e-mail to poeticxpress001@gmail.com for any further communication or feedback.

www.ingramcontent.com/pod-product-compliance
Lightning Source LLC
Chambersburg PA
CBHW051602010526
44118CB00023B/2792